Setting Up Themed Aquariums
Aquariums
Fish and Plants in Harmony

> Axel Gutjahr

Contents

Attractive Community Aquariums

Tanks with Species from One Geographical Region

Summary of Important Points

Selecting Tank and Equipment

There are many reasons for deciding to set up an aquarium. Maybe you have succumbed to the fascination of those display aquariums that you saw when visiting a zoo. But it is also possible that you have given in to secret yearnings for the tropics, or quite simply that you wanted to have a "piece of nature" in your home.

Buying a Tank

No matter what the reason for setting up such a small underwater world, there are a few preliminary, fundamental considerations that need to be taken into account. For instance, you have to assess whether you have a solid enough piece of furniture in your home that will support the weight of such an aquarium. Otherwise, it is advisable

to buy a suitable aquarium display case (or a stand with matching canopy) at the same time you buy the actual tank.

The aquarium trade offers numerous aquarium models, including some futuristic ones, so you will certainly find your desired "dream aquarium." However, before you decide on a model with arched side panels, please remember that these will give you only distorted views of your underwater world. Furthermore, if possible, do not acquire a tank with a volume of less than 16 gallons (60 L), because contrary to popular opinion, small aquariums require relatively more maintenance than large ones. Moreover, when buying an aquarium tank, make sure that the glass is free of scratches, has no tiny internal air bubbles, and that the sides are properly glued together. It is also advisable to test the selected tank with some gentle knocking, to make sure that there are absolutely no tiny cracks in the glass sides and bottom.

> *With correct water chemistry values the fish tend to do well, so the aquarium brings nature a little closer to your home.*

Aquarium Equipment

Many beginning aquarists ask what kind of equipment is absolutely essential for their aquarium. In most instances a combination filter—aerator, a heater with built-in contact thermometer, as well as appropriate lighting, will already be sufficient.

Filter: Outside filters have proven to be very useful, because, contrary to inside filters, they do not impinge on the total water volume of the aquarium. Moreover, they are usually very easy to clean and service, without making a big mess.

Heater: If at all possible you should select a bottom heater. This type may be somewhat more expensive than a simple rod heater, but it does offer a significant advantage—it also provides optimum heating for the bottom substrate, so that the water plants have constantly "warm feet," which will ensure better plant growth.

Lighting: In order to achieve optimum plant growth, efficient lighting is essential. For this, fluorescent tubes are better suited than mercury vapor (high-pressure) lamps.

How to attach the equipment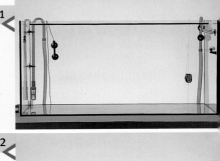

Set up the tank in the location where it is to remain permanently. Install the filter suction pipe and the aerator line. After that, attach the aquarium heater.

Placing the substrate on the bottom

Install the back wall decoration inside the tank. Then place the substrate (after it has been rinsed in running water) on the bottom. A layer of 1½ to 2 inches (3.5 to 5 cm) thick is sufficient in most cases.

Add the water plants

Start decorating the aquarium with roots (bogwood or driftwood), palm leaves, rocks, and/or caves. Add some water to the tank, and then start "planting" the selected plants. Then fill the aquarium with water to within ¾ inch (1.5 cm) of the top.

Conditioning the tank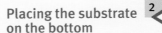

Once these tasks are done, turn the equipment on and operate the aquarium for about three weeks with only a few fish in it. During this period check the water values on a regular basis. As soon as these have stabilized you can introduce fish to the aquarium.

Bottom Substrate and Decoration

Bottom Substrate

In some way the bottom substrate is really part of the decoration because it contributes significantly to a naturelike appearance of the underwater landscape. Beyond that, it fulfills other important functions. For instance, it provides anchorage as well as nutrients for many plants. Furthermore, it offers certain fish suitable spawning opportunities.

Apart from a layer of sand with a slight clay content (covered by a 1 to 1¼-inch- (2 to 3-cm-) thick layer of fine-grained, well-rounded gravel), you can also use *Laterite* as a suitable bottom substrate. This is a nutrient-rich aquarium substrate, available from aquarium shops. It has a reddish to reddish brown color, which is indicative of its high iron content. Certain fish, for instance killifish, require a specific substrate. In order to accommodate them, the bottom should be covered partially or completely with well-washed peat moss.

Yet, other species, for instance many dwarf cichlids, prefer an aquarium where the bottom substrate is covered by fallen leaves from tropical trees.

Decoration

Rocks/Stones: the most frequently used decorative items are without doubt stones and rocks of different sizes and colors. When selecting rocks it is important to pick those that do not have any sharp edges and where the surface areas do not show the presence of embedded mineral or metallic inclusions.

> ## ¹ Coconuts
The half-shells of coconuts, for instance, are ideal hiding— and spawning—places for dwarf cichlids and various small catfish species.

> ## ² Stones
Rocks and stones that are used for making caves and castles must be well glued together, so that they do not collapse.

> ## ³ Roots
Submerged roots give the underwater landscape a naturelike character, and they also function as sight barriers and territorial borders.

8

Calcium-containing stones and rocks are not suitable for most aquarium types because this leads invariably to a severe increase in pH value. Flat stones can readily be assembled into various cave-like structures, provided they are glued together firmly, using silicon sealant. Purchase only aquarium-approved cements at your aquarium store. Additional stability of such caves can be provided by "gluing" them to a slate tile. However, for that purpose, sharp edges of the slate piece need to be covered with sand or gravel.

Roots : Gnarled bogwood roots, as well as roots from African *Mopani* Trees, often give underwater landscapes a very characteristic appearance. However, it is very important that before introducing this type of wood into the tank, it must first be well-soaked in water for two to three weeks.

Caves: Coconut half-shells (cleaned of all copra inside) can make very desirable hiding places as well as spawning sites for many fish. The same applies to bamboo tubes, which should be

> *A dark bottom substrate enhances the coloration of many fish.*

attached in a horizontal position inside the tank.

Other decor: Also very decorative are thin bamboo sticks, but to prevent them from floating up to the surface, they need to be securely attached vertically into some heavy, inert base plate. In order to not spoil the aesthetic appearance of the aquarium, such a base plate should be buried in the substrate. Fish that live among tropical leaves on the bottom should be provided with clean, dry palm leaves, available from florists and similar places.

Dark Bottom Substrate

Dark bottom substrates have proven to be very effective in aquarium keeping.

✔ A dark substrate contributes significantly to making fish feel notably more secure. They show this by displaying more intensive coloration, which then, in most species, becomes even more conspicuous over a dark bottom substrate.

✔ Only for black or almost black fish, respectively, such as Black Mollies, is a light-colored substrate more effective.

✔ A dark substrate can also highlight the coloration of aquarium plants.

Fish in the Aquarium

Correct Aquarium Stocking Density

Many aquarists make the mistake of putting too many fish into their tanks, but it must always be remembered, when a stocking density is too high it tends to cause permanent stress in the fish. This, in turn, weakens their immune system to a point where they become more prone to diseases than fish kept under more favorable conditions. In order to avoid this, it is advisable to determine the number of fish that can be kept in an aquarium, according to the following rule-of-thumb: for a well-aerated and properly planted tank, one should consider about 1 quart (1L) of aquarium water per approximately 2 quarts per 1 inch (2.5 cm) of fish length. For example, a 16-gallon (60-L) aquarium, less 2½ gallons (10 L) of displacement for bottom substrate and decoration, can then accommodate 10 fish of about 2 inches (5 cm) each.

Beyond that, it is important to make sure that a particular tank—in terms of its length and width ratio—is indeed suitable for accommodating certain types (body shapes) of fish. The relationship of length to width, to the body length of particular fish should be approximately 10 : 5 : 1 for particularly active (fast-swimming) types such as Zebra Fish. For less active species, for instance, dwarf labyrinth fish, a ratio of about 8 : 4 : 1 is suitable.

When acquiring juvenile fish you must not consider their current size for the calculation of stocking density, but their ultimate, adult length. In the final analysis, we must always keep in mind the well-established theorem of "less is more". It is better to do without a couple of specimens, thus creating condi-

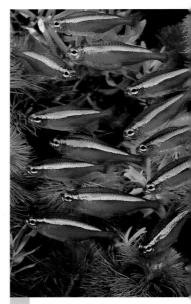

> *Some species, such as Cardinal Tetras, prefer to live in schools (shoals).*

1 Crystalwort

Flowing Crystalwort is a versatile water plant. It is often placed in thick wads ("cushions") onto the bottom (substrate) of a tank.

2 Laceplant

Because of its "perforated," sensitive leaves, the Lace Plant (*Aponogeton madagascariensis*) is suitable only for tanks with peaceful fish.

3 Mexican Oakleaf

With sufficient lighting, the Mexican Oakleaf (*Shinnersia rivularis*) is an extremely rapidly growing plant.

tions that are substantially better for the well-being of the (remaining) fish.

Plants

Water plants are an important component of the natural habitat of fish. They provide hiding places and spawning sites, and sometimes they are even used as food by fish. The most important purpose, however, is their function of enriching the water with oxygen produced during photosynthesis. The oxygen, released this way into the water, is absorbed by fish through their gills and so is used for respiration.

In addition, plants remove excess nutrients from aquarium water and from the bottom substrate. This nutrient is required by the plants for growth and reproduction. Should you notice that plant growth appears to be stagnating in your tank, in spite of adequate lighting, it may be possible that nutrients are no longer present in the aquarium in sufficient quantities. In that case, you will need to fertilize the water plants with commercially available fertilizers. You can also use small clumps of clay that you can form yourself— ½ to ¾ inches (1 to 1.5 cm) in diameter. Then press these into the bottom substrate.

Aquarium plants can be broadly categorized

as follows:
➤ Floating plants, which are not anchored into the substrate and remain free-floating in the tank.
➤ Plants for places in the foreground of the aquarium.
➤ Plants for the middle section of the aquarium that reach only a medium size.
➤ Plants for the background of the aquarium. These are mainly large, bulky plants.
➤ Plants that can be attached permanently to decorative items. Initially such plants must be tied to objects on which they are supposed to grow. Once these plants have become firmly attached to the substrate they no longer need to be anchored.

11

Planting the Aquarium

Before you begin planting your aquarium it is advisable to actually make a planting sketch. Ideally, this should also include major decorative objects to be used in developing the underwater landscape.

Prior to placing individual plants into the tank, any dead or dying leaves should be carefully and gently removed, and large roots, runners as well as newly developing plants, should be trimmed off. The entire root system of each plant is then inserted into a small hole, made by pressing a finger into the substrate. When the plant is properly positioned, the surrounding substrate is slightly compressed over the roots and around the base of the plant.

Snails: When purchasing new aquarium plants, it is important to remember that there are often gelatinlike, barely visible snail eggs attached to the plants, which will soon give rise to baby snails. Initially, these snails will feed on leftover food particles, algae, and wilted leaves of water plants. However, sooner or later, the day will come when the snails start to multiply and their current food supply becomes inadequate; then they will start to gnaw on the healthy aquarium plants. Bushy, fine-feathered plants are then often relentlessly decimated, and plants with large leaves often start to show a multitude of small holes, as signs of the snails' feeding activities. If such a "snail invasion" is to be avoided right from the start, newly acquired plants should be placed in a separate tank for two to three weeks, and a snail removal agent be added to the water. Such preparations are available from most aquarium shops.

> *With a wide array of leaf shapes and colors, water plants create a diversified underwater world.*

Popular Aquarium Plants

Name	Remarks
Dwarf Spearhead *Anubias barteri var.nana*	Distribution: West Africa. Robust and hardy, but slow-growing plant that is easy to attach to rocks and roots.
Crinkled Aponogeton *Aponogeton crispus*	Distribution: Southern India to Sri Lanka. Compact, tall species with undulating leaf margin. This species prefers weakly acidic water and temperatures from 77 to 86°F (25 to 30°C).
African Water Fern *Bolbitis heudelotii*	Distribution: In many areas of Africa. Requires acidic, very soft water. This fern will also thrive under low light levels.
Fanwort *Cabomba caroliniana*	Distribution: Southern United States to South America. The 3.5-foot-(1-m)-long stems of this easy-to-care for, rapidly growing species, should be planted in groups to create large consolidated bushes.
Indian Fern *Ceratopteris thalictroides*	Distribution: Southeast Asia to Australia. The (40 cm) long leaves will readily break off. This plant should not be used for aquariums accommodating digging, burrowing, or otherwise unruly fish.
Crypotocoryne walkeri x nevillii	Hybrid; not a naturally occurring plant. This robust, but slow-growing plant reaches a maximum height of only 3 inches (8 cm).
Amazon Swordplant *Echinodorus amazonicus*	Distribution: Amazon region. Maximum height 20 inches (50 cm). This plant prefers nutrient-rich substrate and weakly acidic water.
Canadian Waterweed *Elodea canadensis*	Distribution: originally North America, now established worldwide. Prefers temperatures below 72° F (22°C) and a pH value of just over 7.0. Contributes strongly to water cleanliness.
Giant Hygrophila *Hygrophila corymbosa*	Distribution: Southeast Asia. Distance between adjacent plants must not be too narrow, or the lower plant stems tend to become bare quickly.
Water Purslane *Ludwigia palustris*	Distribution: Originally North America, now introduced worldwide. Requires a lot of light. With sufficient tank lighting the green leaves will often turn red.
Java Fern *Microsorum pteropus*	Distribution: Tropical Asia. Relatively hardy plant; maximum height 1 foot (30 cm); will also grow under low light levels, but correspondingly slower.
Parrotfeather Watermilfoil *Myriophyllum aquaticum*	Distribution: Originally South America, but now introduced into many other regions. Prefers weakly acidic water, temperatures below 77° F (25°C) and requires high light levels.

Questions and Answers on Aquarium Layout, Using Plants and Decorative Materials

What is meant by a community tank?

To a certain extent a community tank always represents a compromise solution, because it is used for keeping a "community" of fish and plants from totally different regions on earth. In such a situation it is therefore rare that the environmental parameters prevailing in the tank are optimal for each fish and for each plant—something not absolutely required for maintaining a successful community aquarium. It is more important that all aquarium inhabitants find largely suitable aquarium conditions and that all are able to get along with each other.

What is required to prepare bamboo sticks before placing them inside an aquarium?

Aquarium stores often have bamboo sticks for sale, which are more than 3.3 feet (1 m) long. Here the first thing required is to cut them into suitable lengths. In order to avoid fungus, bacteria, and other contaminants from becoming established later on the surface areas of the cuts, it is important to seal them properly. For that purpose we use the well-established method with fiberglass resin or inert alkali silicate sealant (also commonly known as "water glass"). Nowadays, a more appropriate method involves the use of aquarium silicon sealant. Prior to applying the sealant to the cuts, they must be thoroughly cleaned of any residual sawdust. After that, a drying period of at least 24 hours is needed. As already mentioned on Page 9, the use of bamboo sticks inserted in holes made in some inert base plate (which is then buried in the substrate) has proven to be very effective. Another variant of this is gluing a few stones together into a small pile or into a group, for

Plants that have grown too closely together need to be pruned occasionally.

attaching the bamboo sticks between the stones. If this group of stones looks simply too "naked," it can readily be covered—partially or completely—with a bunch of Java Fern. An interesting color alternative to commonly used yellow bamboo sticks, can be brown bamboo, often referred to as "pepper tubes."

What opportunities are there to create an aquarium background ?

Anyone who wants a naturally appearing aquarium should not be satisfied with a wallpaperlike pattern as aquarium background. The aquarium trade offers a wide range of photographs of magnificent underwater landscapes transferred onto plastic foil. These are simply attached to the outside of the aquarium's back window. Also available are plastic recreations of certain sections of river-and-stream banks, for instance, rather naturally appearing rock and root formations. These plastic, embossed "*reliefs*" of river bank profiles are placed inside the tank, just in front of the back window. In days gone by, when these types of manufactured background

decoration were not yet available, aquarists often resorted to simply painting the back of their tanks green. However, this method is definitely not advisable, because once the paint is dry, it tends to create additional structural tension on the glass, which, in the worst-case scenario, can cause the aquarium glass to crack.

Is it sensible to thin out the aquarium plants periodically?

Once an aquarium is well conditioned and "run in," some plants tend to grow very rapidly; consequently, these plants should be pruned at regular intervals. To do that, don't simply cut off the stems just above the bottom; instead, you need to pull the plants out, including their roots. The latter would otherwise start to decompose and place an undesirable burden on the water quality of the aquarium. Beyond that, you should also sever the links between newly established juvenile plants (runners) and their parent plants, a process that needs to be done very cautiously so as not to injure young plants before they grow stronger.

MY TIPS FOR YOU

Plant Arrangements

➤ Bushy-leafed plants are aesthetically effective when planted in consolidated groups.

➤ Large-leaf plants are very suitable as solitary plants.

➤ Aquariums are particularly attractive when there is a combination of plants that have leaves of different colors and variable shapes.

➤ Do not arrange the plants in straight lines, because this will give your aquarium an unnatural appearance.

➤ Do not place individual plants too close to each other. Make sure they have sufficient space to branch out sideways, as well as being able to grow upward.

➤ When there is insufficient tank lighting, water plants tend to become bare, especially along their lower branches. In that case the plants should be pruned by cutting off the upper part of the stems and then simply replanting them in the substrate.

Attractive Community Aquariums

17-gallon (63-L) Community Aquarium

Baseline Data

As the first example of a theme aquarium, I would like to show you how to set

> *Harlequins are barblike fish that prefer warm water and are quite suited for smaller tanks.*

up a 17-gallon (63-L) community aquarium, which is 24 × 15 × 12 inches (60 × 35 × 30 cm) (length × height × width).

The temperature in this tank is 79° F to 82° F (26°C to 28°C), and the water has a pH value of about 6.5. Filtration is over peat moss. The latter makes the water softer and it also acts, to some extent, as an algae inhibitor.

Tank Layout

In the center of the tank there is a 10-inch-(25-cm-) long root, surrounded by two, approximately 3-inch-(7-cm-) large rocks, as well as one or two small pieces of slate. In addition, the bottom substrate is covered by randomly scattered, small palm leaves. In the back of the tank—on the left side—there is a loosely planted, semicircular stand of *Hygrophila*, taking in to account that sufficient light must always reach the lower stem areas of these plants. Opposite that, on the right side, the tank is planted with Java Fern, which is known, just like *Hygrophila*, to grow very well under aquarium conditions. The leaves of both types of water plants serve as spawning substrate for Harlequins. Females of this species are relatively easy to identify on the basis of their full abdominal region. The spawning behavior of this fish is very interesting: the male will wrap its body halfway around that of the female.

In the foreground of the tank there is a stand of *Cryptocoryne walkeri x nevillii*. The tank's water surface is

---

TIP

Conditioning the Aquarium

➤ After the tank has been decorated and planted, it is advisable to wait at least another three weeks before introducing more than a few fish, even though this may test your patience severely. These three weeks will give the new plants sufficient time to establish their roots in the substrate and to start photosynthesis. In addition, useful bacteria will become established in the aquarium and in the filter (which must be in operation during this period) that will convert the rain or tap water, used for filling the tank, into so-called "aquarium water."

> *Butterfly Dwarf Cichlids from Venezuela are among the most colorful species of aquarium fish.*

covered with Crystalwort, which will gradually provide a carpetlike cover. The Java Fern, about fist-size, is attached with fishing line to the root on the bottom of the tank.

The open, unobstructed area (above the root and the stand of *Cryptocorynes)* serves the agile Harlequins as swimming space. It is advisable to make sure that leaves from the Java Fern as well as those of *Hygrophila* do not gradually grow too far into this open area and so reduce the swimming space available to the fish.

The tree root should be arched, at least in part, so as to provide one small cave that can be used by the Butterfly Cichlids as an intermittent hiding place. Moreover, the root as well as the stones and pieces of slate can also offer potential spawning sites for the cichlids. Butterfly Cichlids tend to frequent the lower water sections of the tank, the Harlequins the middle region, and the Clown Killies prefer to remain close to the water surface, where they are well protected by the floating Crystalwort.

SHOPPING LIST

17-gallon (63-L) tank

✔ One pair Butterfly Dwarf Cichlids (*Mikrogeophagus ramirezi*), about 2½ inches (6 cm) each

✔ One male and two female Clown Killies (*Epiplatys annulatus*), each 1½ to 1¾ inches (3.5 to 4 cm)

✔ 7 Harlequins (*Trigonostigma heteromorpha*), 1½ inches (4 cm) each

✔ 6 Java Fern (*Microsorum pteropus*)

✔ 4 Giant Hygrophila (*Hygrophila corymbosa*)

✔ 1 handful Crystalwort (*Riccia fluitans*)

✔ 1 bunch Java Moss (*Vesicularia dubyana*)

✔ 15 *Cryptocoryne walkeri x nevillii)*

19

35-gallon (128-L) Community Aquarium

Baseline data

In contrast to the 17-gallon (63-L) community aquarium, the 35-gallon (128-L) tank (dimensions 30 × 16 × 16 inches (80 × 40 × 40 cm) covers nearly twice the area of the former. The temperature in this tank should be between 75 and 79° F (24 and 26°C), with a pH value adjusted to 7.2.

Layout

Because of the larger area, we can use more plants as well as other decorative items for the internal layout of this tank.

Decoration and plants: Here we have the obvious opportunity to place an app. 8-inch-long (20-cm) bamboo tube each, horizontally in the left and right tank area, as spawning caves for Bushymouth Catfish. In order to give these "caves" a varied appearance, we arrange 2–3-inch (5–7-cm) stones around one of the tubes. A bunch of Java Moss is attached to the other tube, in such a way that its entrance opening disappears below the moss. Then, two or three oval-shaped rocks (about 6 inches [15 cm] long) are placed on the substrate in the middle of the tank, with two Dwarf Spearhead plants on top of them. In the back of these rocks, as well as to their left and right, we then arrange, in groups, the Acherson's Swordplants (max. height of about 8 inches [20 cm]). The cushions of Crystalwort are secured in front of the rocks, using plant needles. For these plants to develop into

> Plants serve as useful hiding places for fish.

1 Variegated or Variable Platy

These attractive Variegated Platies belong to the same genus as Swordtails and Southern Platies, commonly referred to simply as Platies. When these fish are kept together in the same aquarium they often interbreed, giving birth to viable hybrids.

2 Celebes Rainbowfish

The natural habitat of Celebes Rainbowfish is the island of Celebes (Indonesia), where it occurs mainly in mountain streams with a rocky bottom. Phylogenetically, this species is closely related to common Rainbowfish. Males are more colorful than females, and they also have extended fin tips.

sturdy cushions, they need to be kept for a prolonged period of time in shallow dishes with a water level of only a few millimeters. This way the sprouting sections will grow into each other, thus creating structural stability. As the final step—starting from the sides of the tank where planting was left off—you need to arrange the tall Tape Grass (*Vallisneria americanus*), Mexican Oak and Indian Fern in a semicircle, so as to provide adequate background plant cover. Here we need to remember that it makes sense to organ-ize all these plants into groups (as in nature), instead of intermixing them.

Fish: If algae carpets are starting to form gradually over the rocks and stones, it is advisable not to remove them, because they provide an excellent supplementary diet for platies and catfish. Variegated Platies are avail-able in numerous, differently colored varieties. Unless efforts are to be made to purebreed a particular vari-ety, you can also purchase variably colored specimens, in order to introduce a lot of "color" into the tank. The tank space above the rocks and bamboo tubes provides a lot of unobstructed swim-ming room for agile platies and Celebes Rainbowfish. The latter are also known as so-called "perpetual spawners"—they will deposit eggs almost daily among the dense Java Moss bunches. The sexes of Bushymouth Catfish are easy to distin-guish. From a body length of about 3 inches (7 cm) on, the head region of males begins to develop "side whiskers," which are actually tentacle-like skin growths that are quite prominent.

55-gal (200-L) Community Aquarium

Baseline Data

A tank of this size has the dimension 40 × 20 × 16 inches (100 × 50 × 40 cm). The temperature is 75 to 79° F (24 to 26°C) and the pH value is about 6.7.

Layout

In this tank we use a large bogwood root, which is split forklike, touches the back of the tank, and has two, differentially long, branches extending nearly into the left and right front corner of the tank, respectively.

Plants: The large Egyptian White Water Lily (also know as White Lotus) is planted at the spot where the fork of the bogwood root commences. Because of its magnificently colored leaves, this plant not only provides a color contrast among the water plants, it also functions as a focal point for the viewer. The right background of the tank is planted with dense bushes of Fanwort, while the Amazon Swordplants fill the left back sections of the aquarium. The Dwarf Swordplants, which reach a maximum height of only 4 inches (10 cm) will develop gradually into a lawnlike cover, that provides the decor for the front as well as for the middle part of the tank. The Hornwort is not planted directly into the substrate, because it does not develop proper roots. Instead, it is left drifting freely in the water between the Fanwort and the Hornwort stems, which are in parts growing up and along the water surface, where the current created by the aeration is barely noticeable. This is where the Pearl Gourami male likes to build its bubble nest. Such a nest often has a diameter of more than 8 inches (20 cm).

In the central water regions, Hornwort and Fanwort stems serve as spawning medium for Congo Tetra. With sufficient lighting, Hornwort will prove to be an extremely rapidly growing plant, that removes large amounts of dissolved nutrients from the water every day. For that reason, this plant needs to be trimmed more frequently than most other water plants.

Fish: Congo Tetras are rather active fish, yet they must never be kept together with aggressive species, or they become very shy and will hide throughout the day among the water plants. On the other hand, it is quite normal for Leopard

> *Community aquariums accommodate fish from different geographical regions.*

1 Angelfish

Angelfish also occur in numerous, captive-bred varieties that are distinguished by variable colors and different fins. Adult males can be recognized by a well-developed "forehead hump" above the eyes.

2 Leopard Corydoras Catfish

These small catfish prefer the tank areas close to the bottom. They should always be kept in small groups of at least six specimens. Females have a more massive body than males.

3 Egyptian White Lily, also known as White Lotus

The Egyptian White Lily is in a class of its own. There are also specimens with green leaves as well as with leaves that are sprinkled with multiple colors.

SHOPPING LIST

55-gallon (200-L) tank

Fish

✔ 1 pair Angelfish (*Pterophyllum scalare*), each 5–6 inches (12–14 cm)

✔ 1 pair Pearl Gourami (*Trichogaster leeri*), each 4–5 inches (11–13 cm)

✔ 10 Blue Congo Tetras (*Phenacogrammus interruptus*), each 3½ inches (8 cm)

✔ 8 Leopard Corydoras Catfish (*Corydoras julii*), each 2½ inches (6 cm)

Plants

✔ 20 stems Carolina Fanwort (*Cabomba caroliniana*)

✔ 1 Egyptian White Water Lily or Red Tiger Lotus (*Nymphaea lotus*)

✔ 5 Narrow-leaf Amazon Swordplants (*Echinodorus amazonicus*)

✔ 40 Dwarf Sword Plants (*Echinodorus quadricostatus*)

✔ 10 stems Common Hornwort (*Ceratophyllum demersum*)

Corydoras catfish to withdraw for prolonged periods of time under the root. However, at the latest, at feeding time, the entire Catfish mob will emerge from its hiding place, and then busily search the bottom for food with their tactile barbels. In contrast to this, Angelfish appear almost majestic, when they are swimming calmly through the water. Because of the long-drawn-out, threadlike pelvic fins, beginning hobbyists often mistake Angelfish for Labyrinth Fish, but that is incorrect. Angelfish are a very peaceful cichlid species, which is not always true of Labyrinth Fish.

Questions and Answers About Selecting and Caring for Fish

? Should fish be purchased in pairs only?

No. Although for some species this may be advisable (such as many cichlids and labyrinth fish), in general this is not recommended. Other species, such as most of the barbs and tetras, live in nature in more or less large aggregations or schools. If these fish are kept individually or in pairs only, they are not happy because the usual feeling of "safety in numbers," afforded by living in schools, is absent. When we buy such schooling species it is important to make sure that there is an excess of females. This provides the advantage that those females not yet ready to spawn can withdraw and are not constantly hounded by courting males. Again other fish, for instance most representatives of the cichlid genus *Apistogramma,* do best when kept in a small harem, consisting of one male and two to four adult females. This is the same with many of the *Aphyosemion* killifish, which should only be acquired in "trios"—groups of three (one male and two females).

? Can I use the small organisms that occur in my rainwater barrel as fish food ?

Yes, provided the rainwater barrel does not consist of rusting metal, which could poison your fish. These small organisms that are generally found around the perimeter of the drum are nearly always mosquito larva. They make excellent fish food, eagerly eaten by many fish and even have a stimulating effect on fish breeding. However, one should only ever add as many larvae to the tank as are eaten immediately by the fish, because in warm aquarium water they will quickly develop into adult mosquitos, which could then possibly torment you with their stings.

A diversified diet contributes to the well-being of your fish.

? What do I need to keep in mind when keeping fish together that have not been discussed in this book?

Only keep those fish together that are essentially of the same temperament and disposition—that is, do not keep peaceful species together with those that are aggressive. Beyond that, the general requirements for particular species in regard to water quality parameters, such as temperature and pH value, should be largely similar. Also of great importance is that the respective sizes are compatible. Even among peaceful species that are very large, very small tank inhabitants are often viewed as potential prey and then sooner or later are eaten. If you are already keeping species that like to hide, you may need to provide additional hiding places if you buy new cave dwellers. If you are in any doubt as to which species can be safely housed in a community aquarium, you should consult an expert, such as a local fish breeder. You should always check species compatibility carefully before you add new fish to your home aquarium.

? What do I need to observe when buying fish?

Buy only fish that give the impression of being healthy. All of their fins must be intact, the eyes should be clear, and there must not be any raised scales along the body. Also, do not buy any fish that excrete white feces. That is nearly always an indication of a serious infection or a disease of the digestive tract. And, do not buy fish that exhibit malformations on the mouth and of their backbone. When assessing a fish, you should also check its coloration. Here you must always keep in mind that fish kept in a crowded dealer tank are often stressed, a condition that manifests itself in pale coloration. Moreover, a light tank substrate can also adversely affect fish coloration, which will return to normal once the specimen is placed into a properly set up home aquarium. Finally, the fish must exhibit instant flight reactions as soon as they are removed from the dealer's tank; they must not be lethargic and reluctant to move around. If you are in any doubt about a fish's health, do not buy it.

MY TIPS FOR YOU

The Proper Way to Feed Your Fish

➤ Feed your fully grown fish twice daily; juvenile specimens may need to be fed more frequently (three to six times per day), depending on their size. Feed only as much food as is completely eaten within three minutes.

➤ Establish one fasting day per week for your fish. That is not animal cruelty, but instead prevents the fish from getting too fat and increases their agility as well as their well-being.

➤ Offer a variable diet that should include live food, at least occasionally. That stimulates the hunting instinct and prey capture behavior of your fish.

➤ Compose the diet according to the requirement of particular species. For instance, large fish have a preference for correspondingly larger food items.

➤ In order to prevent food from being sucked into the filter, it should be turned off during feeding times.

➤ Make sure that all of your fish are getting their fair share of the food.

Tanks for Closely Related Species

Livebearing Toothcarps

Baseline Data

As an example of a live-bearer aquarium, the 35-gallon (128-L) tank, with the

> Waterweed is very well suited for tanks with livebearers.

dimensions 30 × 16 × 16 inches (80 × 40 × 40 cm), is used here once again. Many livebearing toothcarp prefer a water temperature that is rather warmer than too cold. Therefore, the temperature in this tank needs to be set to at least 77° F (25°C). The pH

value can range from 7.1 to 7.3.

Layout

Decoration and plants: In one corner of the tank there is a root that extends three branches, fingerlike, into the middle of the tank. In the center of the tank there are five, fist-size, whitish rocks scattered around that provide an attractive contrast to the dark substrate as well as to the three small pieces of slate lying on top of it. In order to further enhance the contrast, we place some cushions of Crystalwort (commonly referred to simply as *Riccia*) between the rocks, securing them with plant needles. Subsequently, arrange in groups and in the back of the tank: Tape grass (*Vallisneria*), thin-stemmed Water Hyacinths—starting on the left side—and followed by Common Water Weed The Water Hyacinths should be placed approximately in the middle of the aquarium to serve as a focal point. In contrast to more or

less spoon-shaped leaves of Water Hyacinths as floating plants, those of the underwater form are more palmleaf-shaped, readily attracting the attention of anyone who looks at the tank. Hornwort is permitted to float freely in the water, where it provides a safe haven for newly born juveniles and those only a few days old.

Fish: Some livebearers, including species such as the Mosquito Fish (*Gambusia holbrooki*), will actively pursue their young as food, but there are others, represented by the Short-finned Molly (*Poecilia sphenops*), that will leave their progeny largely unmolested. However, in the event that "peaceful" species like the latter suddenly start to eat some of their young, this may have to be viewed as a sign of an unbalanced diet that contains too little protein. There is also the popular belief that livebearing toothcarp are typical "beginners' fish." That is not correct. Admittedly, some livebearers

> *Many livebearers also occur as very attractive captive-bred varieties that contribute to the colorful appearance of a tank.*

can more readily cope with small mistakes in their husbandry and care than, for example, Discus Cichlids, but generally they are not as hardy as many egglaying toothcarp. For instance, nearly all livebearing toothcarp (killifish) do not like to be kept in relatively hard water with a pH value that is constantly above 7.0. Moreover, if you set up an aquarium with species that do not prey on their own progeny, this can lead to massive overcrowding.

The water conditions thus created will no longer be suitable for the fish. However, this can readily be avoided with the introduction of one or two Striped Panchax (fish that belong to the group of killifish). These are small predator fish that will make sure that the young born in this tank will not reach maturity. However, Striped Panchax should not be kept together with very small livebearers, because these would also be considered as prey.

SHOPPING LIST

Tank for livebearers

Fish

✔ 6 Southern or Moon Platy *(Xiphophorus maculatus)*, 2 ½ inches (6 cm) each

✔ 6 Guppy *(Poecilia reticulata)*, 1 ½ to 2 inches (3.5 to 5 cm) each

✔ 6 Blackbelly Limia *(Limia melanogaster)*, 2 ½ inches (6 cm) each

Plants

✔ 15 stems Common Waterweed *(Egeria densa)*

✔ 15 Common Tape Grass *(Vallisneria spiralis)*

✔ 3 thin-stemmed Water Hyacinths (Underwater form: *Eichhornia azurea)*

✔ 5–6 cushions Crystalwort *(Riccia fluitans)*

✔ 5–6 stems Common Hornwort *(Ceratophyllum demersum)*

Peaceful Cichlids

To this day there is a belief among aquarium hobbyists that all cichlids are not only aggressive toward each other, but that they also harass other tank inhabitants and that they dig in the bottom substrate with an apparent determination to pull out all water plants. That may be undeniably true for some cichlids, but certainly not for all.

> *"Displaying" males of the Venezuelan Butterfly Dwarf Cichlid.*

Those that have been selected for this tank are indeed largely peaceful. Yet, when one cichlid is guarding its own spawning site and a member of another species approaches too closely, it is vehemently driven off.

First, a remark about the Red Gabon Cichlid: Sometimes, other cichlids, very similar in appearance to the "Gabon" but very aggressive, are being offered for sale as "Gabon Cichlids." Therefore, it is advisable to observe the fish for sale very closely prior to purchase. If they are frequently seen attacking each other aggressively and they have seriously torn fins, they are most likely not "Red Gabons."

Baseline Data:

A tank with the dimensions of 40 × 20 × 16 inches (100 × 50 × 40 cm), with a water temperature of 77 to 81° F (25 to 27°C), and a pH value of 6.8 should be considered suitable, acceptable parameters for this type of cichlid.

Layout:

Decoration and Plants:

Since nearly all cichlids prefer well-structured aquariums, with ample hiding places and appropriate sight barriers, the following tank layout is recommended: two roots are placed toward the back of the tank, with their angular branches protruding into the middle of the tank, where they can partially cross over each other. A rocky cave, which has been glued onto a piece of slate, should be established in the central tank area. Two coconut half-shells "hidden" among Acherson's Swordplants or Congo Water Fern, respectively, are positioned close to the tank's two side panels. The sweeping leaves of Broadleaf Swordplants fill out the left background up to almost the center of the tank. From there the Magenta (or Scarlet) Water Hedge (requiring high light levels for proper growth !) take over. However, it is important that these are not planted too close to each other, or their leaves tend to

1 Butterfly Cichlid (also known as Ram Cichlid)

The Venezuelan Butterfly Cichlid *(Mikrogeophagus ramirezi)* is very intensively colored, but also less robust than the Bolivian Butterfly Cichlid.

2 Red Gabon Cichlid

This is a very easy-to-keep 5-inch-long (12-cm) species, which was discovered only a few years ago. Its name obviously stems from its prominent red color scheme.

3 Purple Cichlid (or Kribensis)

Because of its peaceful nature and beautiful coloration, the Purple Cichlid is very popular. Here the female is always more colorful than the male.

decay due to lack of sufficient lighting. The right side of the tank background is the location for the Giant *Hygrophila*. Among the branches of the roots, as well as in the front area of the tank, we plant a scattered pattern of Cryptocorynes (*C. walkeri x nevillii*). These plants are supposed to gradually grow toward each other and so form a solid "stand" of plants. Monitor their growth.

Labyrinth Fish

Extraordinary Fish

The geographical "home" (center of species abundance) of labyrinth fish is concentrated in the warmer regions of Asia. Their popular name comes from an anatomical peculiarity referred to as the "labyrinth." This is a supplementary respiratory organ, located in the head behind the eyes. This enables labyrinth fish to "breathe" atmospheric air at the water surface. In order to avoid oxygen deficiency in an aquarium for labyrinth fish that could quickly lead to death by asphyxiation, the top of such an aquarium must *never* be covered airtight. Because of the presence of this anatomical feature, a tank with labyrinth fish need not be aerated.

Labyrinth fish usually swim very slowly or often remain stationary in the water for long periods of time. They very much prefer densely planted tanks, where they generally remain among water plants drifting at the surface or, respectively, in a cave, to build their bubble nests. Some labyrinth fish, such as Edith's Fighting Fish, as a mouth brooder, inhabit the lower or middle water regions of the tank. In some species, for instance in Blue Gouramis, males tend to harass females that are not willing to spawn. In order to minimize these attacks it is advisable to spread them out

Blue Gourami do not place particularly high demands on water quality.

Tank for Labyrinth Fish

Fish

- ✔ 1 male and 2 female Blue Gourami (*Trichogaster trichopterus*), 4 to 5 inches (11–12 cm) each
- ✔ 1 Pair Ornate Ctenopoma (*Microctenopoma ansorgii*), 3 inches (7 cm) each
- ✔ 1 Pair Black Paradise Fish (*Macropodus concolor*), 4 inches (11 cm) each
- ✔ 1 male and 2 female Dwarf Gourami (*Colisa lalia*), 2½ inches (6 cm) each
- ✔ 1 Pair Edith's Fighting Fish (*Betta edithae*), 2 to 3 inches (5–7 cm) each
- ✔ 1 Pair Spike-tailed Gourami (*Pseudosphromenus dayi*), 3 inches (7 cm) each

Plants

- ✔ 3 Crinkled Aponogeton (*Aponogeton crispus*)
- ✔ 3 African Fern (*Bolbitis heudelotii*)
- ✔ 3 Java Fern (*Microsorum pteropus*)
- ✔ 2 handfulls Crystalwort (*Riccia fluitans*)
- ✔ 25 stems Giant Ambulia (*Limnophila aquatica*)
- ✔ 1 Egyptian White Water Lily also known as Red Tiger Lotus (*Nymphaea lotus*)
- ✔ 40 stems Pearl Grass (*Hemianthus micranthemoides*)

1 Mouth Brooder

Some labyrinth fish, including Edith's Fighting Fish, do not build bubble nests, because they are mouth brooders. Here, the male takes the eggs into its mouth, immediately after spawning, where they remain for 11 to 13 days. Thereafter, the young will hatch and immediately commence searching for food.

2 Bubble Nest Builder

Among Labyrinth Fish, Dwarf Gourami males build the most artistic bubble nests. There are also several captive-bred varieties of this species available in the aquarium trade. Apart from males that epitomize the original form, where the red and blue components are largely balanced, males from the various varieties usually show an excess of one of these two color components.

(so to speak) over a larger number of females present in the same tank. For that purpose it is advisable to keep at least two or three females per male.

Baseline Data

If you plan to keep some of the large labyrinth fish species, you must provide tank accommodations with the minimum dimensions of 40 × 20 × 16 inches (100 × 50 × 40 cm). The water temperature needs to be 77 to 82° F (25 to 28°C) and there should be a pH value ranging from 6.5 to 7.0.

Layout

Very appropriate for fish from Southeast Asia is the use of bamboo in an aquarium. This type of decoration is most suitable when used as a background. The distance between individual bamboo sticks should be slightly less than 1 inch (about 2 cm). In the left half of the tank you place a small root and on the right side a coconut half shell, which can be used by Spike-tailed Gourami as spawning cave. Crystalwort drifts freely along the water surface. With the exception of the right corner, where Crinkled Aponogeton are located, plant the remainder of the background area (between the groups of bamboo sticks) with Giant Ambulia (*Limnophila aquatica*). The Egyptian White Water Lily is placed in the center of the tank. From the Red Tiger Lotus outward toward the sides of the tank, you should plant, in small groups, African Ferns or Asian Ferns. The tank area towards the front is intended for Pearl Grass.

Small Tetras

The classical fish schools, where all changes of direction and other movements are executed in a synchronized fashion by the entire group, really occur only among marine fish. Among fresh-

The Black (Widow) Tetra (also known as White Skirt Tetra) has been a popular aquarium fish for many years.

water fish, however, the behavior of many small tetras (such as the Cardinal Tetra

[*Paracheirodon axelrodi*]) comes fairly close to those traditional fish schools in the marine environment. Nearly all tetras do particularly well when they are able to form large congregations. Under aquarium conditions even different tetra species can join together to form such large groups. In order to cater to such well-defined group association behavior, tetras must never be kept as individual specimens. Instead, there must always be at least five or six (preferably more) specimens of one particular species in an aquarium. In contrast to most of the South American tetras, which are generally rather actively swimming fish, there are also more sedate and slow-moving tetras from Africa. Characteristic, however, for all species is that they are largely peaceful toward other tank inhabitants. Therefore, tetras must never be kept together with aggressive fish, because that would cause permanent stress to the tetras and they would become

frightened and hide among water plants and other items of tank decorations.

Baseline Data

If you plan to keep a school of tetras, you must provide tank accommodations with the minimum dimensions of 32 × 16 × 16 inches (80 × 40 × 40 cm). The water temperature needs to be 75 to 78° F (24 to 26°C), and there should be a pH value of 6.5 to 6.7.

Layout

Decoration and Plants: The entire bottom substrate should be covered with a mixture of fibrous peat moss and an ample amount of palm leaves. Often peat moss will create a slight brownish (tea-colored) tinge in the water, but this should not be viewed as a problem—quite the contrary. Under natural environmental conditions many natural bodies of water inhabited by tetras are of similar coloration. Yet, anyone who rather prefers totally clear water in the tank, needs only to use activated carbon

as a filter medium, and the colored substances are quickly filtered out of the water. If, on the other hand, you want brownish aquarium water permanently, you will, after the initial water changes, need to add some peat extract to the tank. Such peat extract can either be home-made or purchased in an aquarium shop. Close to the back wall of the tank place a large root, so that a substantial open space is being created in front of it; it is then filled with scattered plantings of Dwarf Swordplants. This open space becomes the swimming area for the tetras. On the left side, next to the root, plant Amazon Swordplants as well as Java Fern in groups, arranged in an approximate semicircle. For that, the shorter Java Fern is placed in front of the Amazon Swordplants. To the right of the root, and also in a semicircle, plant Sumatra Fern as well as bunches of Fanwort. Tetras utilize these fine feathery plants as spawning medium. Along the surface distribute Hooded Floating Fern, which requires a very large amount of light. At the same time, it creates sub-

> *A school of small tetras swims peacefully through aquarium plants.*

dued lighting in the lower tank region. This not only enhances the coloration of tetras, but the fish also feel much safer when the lighting is less bright.

Fish: The black and silvery white Black (Widow) Tetra provides an excellent contrast to the red and black of Flame Tetras, as well as to the delicate yellow and blue, displayed by the Congo Tetras. Apart from the coloration of fish, the variable body shapes of different species also make for interesting, contrast-rich appearances.

SHOPPING LIST

Tetra Tank

✔ 6 Flame Tetra (*Hyphesso-brycon flammeus*), 1 ½ inches (4 cm) each

✔ 6 Black (Widow) Tetra (*Gymnocorymbus ternetzi*), 2 ¼ inches (6 cm) each

✔ 6 Yellow Congo Tetra (*Alestopetersius caudalis*), 3 inches (7 cm) each

✔ 40 Dwarf Swordplants (*Echinodorus quadricostatus*)

✔ 4 Indian Fern (*Ceratopteris thalictroides*)

✔ 4 Amazon Swordplant (*Echinodorus amazonicus*)

✔ 20 stems Fanwort (*Cabomba caroliniana*)

✔ 30 Hooded Floating Fern (*Salvinia cucullata*)

✔ 8 Java Fern (*Microsorum pteropus*)

Barbs and Barblike Fish

Baseline Data

For the fast-swimming, agile barbs and barblike fish native to Africa and Asia, we select a 55-gallon (200-L) tank with the dimensions of 40 × 20 × 16 inches (100 × 50 × 40 cm). The water temperature ranges from 72 to 79° F (22 to 26°C) and the pH value is set at 6.5. The water can be filtered over fibrous peat moss.

Rosy Barbs can also be kept in a garden pond during the summer months.

Layout

Decoration and Plants:

The bottom substrate consists of fine-grained material that must not contain sharp, angular gravel, which could injure the tank inhabitants when they are digging in the substrate in search of food. The background decoration consists of several groups of thin bamboo sticks, positioned strategically among the plants. We distribute 8 to 10 fist-sized rocks over the substrate, toward the front and central portion of the tank. Among them we attach cushions of Crystalwort, with the aid of plant needles. Java Fern is attached to rocks using thin fishing line. These particular plants, together with bunches of Asian Marshweed are the preferred spawning substrate for these fish. Asian Marshweed bunches are placed immediately in front of the crinkled Aponogetons that are arranged in a semicircle in the left, far corner of the tank. In the back of the Aponogeton we plant giant

Tank for Barbs and Barblike Fish

Fish
- ✔ 10 Zebra Fish *(Danio rerio)*, 5–5¼ inches (12.5–13 cm) each
- ✔ 8 Rosy Barb *(Puntius conchonius)*, 3–3¼ inches (7–8 cm) each
- ✔ 10 Barred Barbs *(Barbus fasciolatus)*, 2 inches (5 cm) each

Plants
- ✔ 15 stems Asian Marshweed *(Limnophila sessiliflora)*
- ✔ 5 Water Wisteria *(Hygrophila difformis)*
- ✔ 7 Giant Hygrophila *(Hygrophila corymbosa)*
- ✔ 4 Crinkled Aponogeton *(Aponogeton crispus)*
- ✔ 2 bunches Java Moss *(Vesicularia dubyana)*
- ✔ 7–8 Cuchions Crystalwort *(Riccia fluitans)*

Other items
- ✔ 8 Bamboo sticks
- ✔ 8–10 rocks, fist-size

Hygrophila, fairly close to the back wall of the tank. All of these plants extend almost into the right far corner of the tank where Water Wisteria is being arranged so that it does not fill out the corner only, but also grows

1 Zebra Fish

The Zebra Fish belongs to the more robust barb-like fish and can even be kept outdoors in a garden pond during the summer months. Moreover, compared to some of the other species, it is very easy to breed and therefore it is ideal for those hobbyists who wish to obtain experience in breeding barblike fish.

2 Asian Marshweed

Many barbs and barblike fish prefer to spawn in such fine feathery plants, and also occasionally "nibble" on the leaves. Consequently, Asian Marshweed , which occurs in slow-flowing rivers in southern and southeast Asia, is well suited for use in tanks with barbs.

along the side window, slightly toward the front of the tank.

Fish: By cleverly grouping the decor items and the plants, a large open swimming space is created in the center and front of the tank, where these agile fish can readily "romp around." Beyond that, it is important to point out, that barbs and barblike fish should always be kept in groups, made up of at least five or six specimens each. Here it is also very important to remember that each group of fish should always include a few males. Without the presence of males, females cannot expel their eggs, which tends to lead to the condition known as "egg binding." When this happens, eggs that are not released will degenerate in the ovaries, causing metabolic disturbances as well as inflammations that will often lead to the demise of the affected female.

In this context it must also be noted here that in a well-stocked aquarium—even after a successful spawning—one should not expect any progeny. The reason for this is that all barbs and barblike fish are aggressive egg predators that will invariably find most of the eggs they have laid. When keeping barbs and barblike fish, one should also include some vegetable matter in their normal diet, such as finely chopped lettuce. Otherwise, the fish can develop an incredibly good appetite and will then start nibbling on the more delicate aquarium plants.

Egglaying Toothcarps ("Killifish")

Killifish

Egglaying toothcarps occur in a variable number of species in (southern) Europe, Africa, Asia, South America, and North America. They are often simply called Killis or Killifish; this is not a reference to the word "*kill*," but instead it has its origin in the Dutch word "*kil*," which means "small body of water." It characterizes the preferred habitat of these fish. Hardly any other fish group has developed so many different spawning strategies in the course of its evolution as killifish have.

Apart from species that attached their eggs to fine feathery plant leaves or on to the roots of floating plants, there are those that bury the abdominal portion of their body (or even the entire body) into soft-bottom substrate to deposit their eggs. Males of the American Flag Fish (*Jordanella floridae*) practice what may be a preliminary stage of brood care among killifish, whereby a day after spawning, they commence producing a slight water current—with their fins—over the clutch of eggs.

In essence then, when setting up a killifish tank you have to take into account not only the behavior of individual species, but also the various spawning strategies practiced by them, particularly, the males of some species are rather aggressive toward their own siblings. Fortunately, however, the "combatants" rarely ever sustain any serious injuries, and slightly torn fins generally heal quickly. Some species, for instance, such as *Guenther's Nothobranchius*, have the distinct disadvantage of not getting very old.

1 Red-lined Killifish

In contrast to simple beige-colored females, males of this *Aphyosemion* species are extremely colorful.

2 Red-chinned Panchax

This killifish is a robust, easy-to-care-for species, which is readily available in well-established aquarium shops.

3 Guenther's Nothobranchius

This species originates in East Africa, where it frequently lives in small standing waters with a muddy bottom.

Baseline Data

The killifish fish tank discussed here has the dimensions 32 × 16 × 16 inches (80 × 40 × 40 cm); the temperature is 72 to 75° F (22 to 24°C) and the pH value is 6.5.

Layout

The tank bottom is covered with fine sand, but only in the back section, while we place a 8 cm wide and 6 cm deep layer of fibrous peat moss along the front window, as spawning substrate for the "diving" Nothobranchius and Aphyolebias (Longfins) species. In the two back corners there are two bogwood roots that have branches extending into the middle of the tank, possibly (partially) crossing over each other. In addition, several fist-size rocks are scattered along the bottom of the tank. Attach Dwarf Spearhead to the rock in front of the tank, using thin fishing line. Crystalwort, which serves as cover and spawning substrate for Red-chinned Panchax, is left floating along the surface. The remainder of the plants are located exclusively in the sandy section of the substrate, and the Broad-leaf Sword-plants as well as bunches of

> Newly planted Java Fern; later on the leaves will split up in an antlerlike fashion.

Cabomba caroliniana fill out the back section of the tank. In front of them, we distribute the Java Ferns, so that four of these plants are flanked by extensions (branches) from the root.

The "plant jungle" thus created and the various items of decoration are there mainly to provide nonspawning females with appropriate hiding places, so that they are—at least intermittently—able to escape from constantly courting males. This is very important to their health.

Killifish Tank

✔ 1 male and 2 female Red-lined Killifish (Aphyosemion striatum), 2 inches (5 cm) each

✔ 8 Guenther's Nothobranchius (Nothobranchius guentheri), 1–1½ inches (3.5–4 cm) each

✔ 1 male and 2 female Red-chinned Panchax (Epiplatys dageti monroviae), 3–4 inches (8–10 cm) each

✔ 1 male and 2 female Peruvian Longfin (Aphyolebias peruensis), 3–4 inches (8–10 cm) each

✔ 2 handful Crystalwort (Riccia fluitans)

✔ 7 Java Fern (Microsorum pteropus)

✔ 20 stems Fanwort (Cabomba caroliniana)

Behavior Interpreter
Aquarium

Many types of behavior can be observed in an aquarium. Here you find out, what fish are trying to express with their behavior ❓ and how you respond to it correctly ➡.

> Swordtails feeding on a food tablet.

❓ These fish are feeding harmoniously in a group

➡ Please do not feed too much, or the fish become fat and lethargic.

> Two Siamese Fighting Fish males in combat.

❓ These fish always enter into extremely aggressive territorial fights.

➡ The males must be separated, because such a fight is inevitably fatal for one of them.

This is a labyrinth fish building a nest made of bubbles along the surface.

❓ This nest is used subsequently for holding the eggs during their development.

➡️ Turn the aquarium aeration lower so that the nest will not be destroyed.

Male paradise fish draping its body in a semicircle around that of the female.

❓ This is a phase of the normal spawning behavior.

➡️ Please, do not disturb. The male will eventually release the female again.

A catfish digging in the substrate in search of food.

❓ This is quite a common, natural behavior.

➡️ Avoid using gravel with sharp angular edges that can injure the fish.

Dwarf cichlid males displaying to each other.

❓ This behavior serves to demonstrate strength toward an opponent.

➡️ If this leads to an actual fight it is advisable to separate the fish.

41

Questions and Answers About Caring for an Aquarium

In what time intervals do I have to do a general cleaning of the aquarium?

For a well-conditioned aquarium, one that is being correctly serviced and regularly attended to, this may be only required every one to three years. However, in order to achieve such long intervals between major cleaning work, you need to service the aquarium on a weekly basis. The principal task involved here is to change at least a quarter of the water by siphoning it out of the tank. At the same time you should also remove (siphon out) sed-iments that have accumulated on the bottom as well as pos-sible algal patches (layers) that become established on the glass and on the tank dec-oration. Also, the filter needs to be thoroughly cleaned; the tank substrate (which usually becomes compacted as time goes on) should be loosened with a rod or spatula. If need be, some of the plants can also be thinned out. In a broader sense, correct feeding and sensible tank lighting of 12 to 14 hours daily must also be considered as part of the routine (daily) aquarium care. Fluorescent tubes will gradually lose light intensity and should be replaced with new ones every six to nine months.

What is meant by pH value?

The pH value is the nega-tive, common logarithm of the hydrogen concentration in water. Expressed in simpler terms: the pH value indicates whether particular substances react acidic, alkaline, or neu-tral. With a pH value of 7 there is an identical concen-tration of hydrogen ions (H^+) and hydroxide ions (OH^-) and the water reacts neutral. If, however, there is an access of hydrogen ions, the pH val-ue drops below 7.0 and the water shows an increasingly acid reaction. Inversely, when the pH value increases above 7.0 with an increased concen-tration of hydroxide ions, the water takes on an increasingly alkaline character. Instead of

Black Mollies like to feed on green algae, but only to a lim-ited extent.

talking about an alkaline character, one can also refer to this as a basic character or reaction.

The pH value of aquarium water can be determined with the aid of a commercially available test strip. If you wish to spend a little more money, you can also purchase a high-precision, electronic device for measuring the pH.

My aquarium is almost totally overgrown by green algae. What can I do about it?

Green algae only develop in excess when they find favorable environmental conditions. This is exactly the point at which you need to start your "attack." Especially during the summer months, many tanks are exposed to long and intensive solar radiation (sunshine), that tends to stimulate the growth of green algae. Therefore, the room where the aquarium is located should be darkened every day for a few hours by pulling down the shades, but it must not be completely dark. Furthermore, the food supply of the algae, which consists principally of nutrients dissolved in the tank water, must be substantially reduced. That can be achieved by generous, partial water changes, which should be done at least every two days. This procedure should be viewed as a short-term (emergency) procedure only until the nutrient level has been sufficiently reduced in the tank.

Finally, there is the biological removal of algae. For that purpose we place a handful of dry barley or wheat straw into a nylon bag, which is then placed inside the aquarium. The straw gives off substances that will quickly kill most green algae species, but at the same time it is totally harmless to fish and higher plants. When, after one to two weeks, all algae have disappeared, the bag with the straw can be removed. Following that, at least 90% of the tank water needs to be replaced with fresh (well-conditioned and NOT straight from the tap) water. This procedure is very important in order to reduce the dissolved nutrients that have been generated by the dying and decaying algae. If this water change is not done, the nutrients present at that stage in abundance in the water often serve as the basis for a renewed green algae "explosion."

MY TIPS FOR YOU

Check the Health of Your Fish Every Day

➤ Every day, preferably in the morning, when all your fish appear healthy and are swimming normally, make sure that the technical components of your tank are all operating correctly and that the water temperature is as required.

➤ If some of the fish seem to behave in an abnormal fashion, for instance, if they are constantly at the water surface, gasping for air, or they exhibit no interest in food that they normally eat eagerly, these are often signs of the onset of a disease.

➤ Small white dots, distributed in an irregular pattern over the body and fins of the fish, are a sign of a disease. Immediately contact your aquarium or appropriate pet shop dealer for professional advice.

➤ Treat only diseased fish with medication, and never add medication as a prophylaxis. Such permanent exposure to medication, not needed for actual treatment, will often weaken the immune system of the fish.

43

Tanks with Species from One Geographical Region

South American Tank

A large number of fish suitable for a South American tank come from the Amazon River and its multitude of tributaries. There, in many areas, fallen leaves and other decomposing plant matter provide a soft bottom substrate in these jungle waters, from which dead tree roots and branches protrude.

Baseline Data

This particular suggestion for a theme aquarium for a South American tank is based on the dimensions of 40 × 20 × 16 inches (100 × 50 × 40 cm). The water temperature is 79° F (26° C), with a pH value of 6.5.

Lay-out

Decoration and Plants: In this South American tank, distribute a mixture of fibrous peat moss and small, chopped-up palm leaves over a fine-grained substrate. These are all materials among which *Corydoras* catfish and many dwarf cichlids like to hide intermittently. In the center of the tank there is a large root. In the front (and to the right of it), as well as on the left (in the back of it), bury one coconut half-shell each in the substrate, so that only a small entrance gap is available to the "Agassiz's" females for access. In such narrow-entrance spawning caves, these dwarf cichlids feel particularly safe. Amazon Frogbit, floating at the sur-

face, creates subdued lighting in the lower tank regions. Behind and in the back of the root you plant palmlike, thin-stemmed Water Hyacinths as well as Fanwort. These should be flanked—right and left—by two or three Broad-leaf Swordplants. The front area of the tank is decorated with Dwarf Swordplants, which are initially scattered about loosely , but will eventually form a lawnlike cover. In the area to either side of the root you should place groups of attractive Ascherson's Sword-plants.

Fish: Because of its fish composition, this South American tank gives off an atmosphere of tranquility. Tetras and angelfish move leisurely through the tank, and the Agassiz male often remains motionless in the water or patrols slowly through its territory. It can even be exciting to watch when the dwarf cichlid females leave their caves, meeting and threatening each other, or a group of Bandit (*Corydoras*) catfish emerges from its hiding place

> *Angelfish are typical inhabitants for a South American tank.*

1 Agassiz's Dwarf Cichlid

This dwarf cichlid is often available in aquarium shops. The substantially larger male is conspicuous by a very attractively colored tail fin.

2 Bandit Catfish

The scientific species name (*metae*) refers to Rio Metae, a river in South America where this species was discovered. In comparison to other *Corydoras* species, this one will readily breed in an aquarium.

3 Bleeding Heart Tetra

This magnificently colored tetra lives primarily in streams with peat moss-containing substrate, in the drainage region of the Upper Amazon River.

SHOPPING LIST

South American Tank

✔ 1 pair Angelfish (*Ptero-phyllum scalare*), 4½–5½ inches (12–14 cm) each

✔ 1 male and 2 female Agassiz's Dwarf Cichlids (*Apistogramma agassizii*), 2–3½ inches (5–9 cm) each

✔ 8 Bleeding Heart Tetras (*Hyphessobrycon erythrostigma*), 3 inches (8 cm) each

✔ 6 Bandit Corydoras Catfish (*Corydoras metae*), 2½ inches (6 cm) each

✔ 20 Amazon Frogbit (*Limnobium laevigatum*)

✔ 30 Dwarf Swordplant (*Echinodorus quadri-costatus*)

✔ 15 stems Fanwort (*Cabomba caroliniana*)

✔ 2 thin-stemmed Water Hyacinth (totally submersed form of: *Eichhornia azurea*)

✔ 5 Broadleaf Swordplant (*Echinodorus bleheri*)

✔ 7 Narrowleaf Swordplant (*Echinodorus ascher-sonianus*)

under the root, to look busily for food along the bottom. However, following a significant, partial water change, a lot of life may become infused in this tank because the added fresh water has a stimulating effect and may induce spawning among catfish and tetras. If so, the fish will commence their intriguing courtship games. When it comes to spawning, the highly active Bandit (*Corydoras*) catfish are not particularly selective; they attach their eggs to plants, decorative components, and even to bare tank glass. Make sure that this does not cause a problem in the aquarium.

Southeast Asian Tank

Some of the more characteristic Southeast Asian fish species include barbs and labyrinth fish. While most

> *Male Tiger Barbs can be recognized by their "red noses."*

barbs are extremely agile fish, labyrinth fish are more quiet and sedate. Nevertheless, some fish from both groups are quite compatible together in a community tank: for example, the not-too-temperamental Black Ruby Barb (*Puntius nigrofasciatus*), which can readily be kept

together with Paradise Fish (*Macropodus*), which are clearly more stress-resistant than Pearl Gouramis (*Trichogaster leeri*).

Baseline data

As an example of a Southeast Asian tank we use a 35-gallon (128-L) aquarium with the dimensions 30 × 16 × 16 inches (80 × 40 × 40 cm). The water temperature is 73 to 75° F (23 to 24°C) and the pH value is 6.8.

Layout

Decoration and Plants: The bottom substrate consists of fine-grained, well-rounded (smooth) sand or gravel that

cannot inflict injuries to fish when they occasionally dig in the substrate in search of food. As decoration we select bamboo sticks, as well as rounded stones of different sizes. The latter are arranged in small groups along the back window of the tank. Some of the stones are also arranged in groups side by side, while others are placed individually or in groups of two or are scattered about over the entire substrate area. Bunches of Java Moss are attached (using very thin fishing line) to one of the groups of stones that should be displaced slightly toward the left, close to the front glass. The

> The very active Black Ruby Barb is a fish that has been popular with aquarium hobbyists for many years.

remainder of the front area of the tank is planted with *Cryptocoryne walkeri x nevillii.* Of course, this particular plant can also be replaced with other species that remains small, such as *Cryptocoryne affinis.* Eared Watermoss, drifting on the surface, serves as spawning substrate for the Striped *Panchax.* Other fish that tend to remain close to the surface also feel safer under such protective cover of floating plants, rather than being so openly exposed in a "naked" aquarium. Moreover, male Paradise Fish like to build their bubble nest among floating plants. The aeration of the tank needs to be turned down though, so that a strong water current along the surface does not destroy the nest. In the far corner, on the left side of the tank, as well as partially along the side window, we plant Giant Hygrophila, while Crinkled Aponogetons are placed in groups in the far right corner. The area between the Hygrophila and the Crinkled Aponogeton can be filled with Asian Fern to fill out the tank plantings.

SHOPPING LIST

Southeast Asian Tank

- ✔ 1 male and 2 female Paradise Fish (*Macropodus opercularis*), 3–4 inches (8–10 cm) each
- ✔ 8 Black Ruby Barbs (*Puntius nigrofasciatus*), 2½ inches (6 cm) each
- ✔ 1 male and 2 female Striped Panchax (*Aplocheilus lineatus*), 4–5 inches (10–12 cm) each
- ✔ 3 small bunches Java Fern (*Vesicularia dubyana*)
- ✔ 15 Eared Watermoss (*Salvinia auriculata*)
- ✔ 6 Giant Hygrophila (*Hygrophila corymbosa*)
- ✔ 25 *Cryptocoryne walkeri x nevillii*
- ✔ 5 Indian Fern (*Ceratopteris thalictroides*)

African Tank

(Lake) Tanganyika and (Lake) Malawi tanks are often given as examples of typical African aquariums. Yet, because of the very high (alkaline) pH values that need to prevail in these aquariums, such tanks are really only suitable for a small portion of African freshwater fish.

Baseline Data

For that reason none of these (lake-) type aquariums will be represented here, but instead an aquarium where the pH value is "only" 6.5 to 6.8, together with a water temperature of 80° F (27°C). This tank has the dimensions of $40 \times 20 \times 16$ inches ($100 \times 50 \times 40$ cm).

Layout

Decoration and Plants: You should distribute an ample amount of palm leaves over the bottom substrate. A large, very gnarled *Mopani* Tree root is placed in the center of the tank. To this you attach four of the Dwarf Spearheads, using very thin fishing line. In front of the root you place a slate tile, which—together with the other three flat rocks that are distributed along the tank floor—can be used by cichlids as a spawning site.

Sometimes, however, Red Gabon Cichlids prefer to spawn in the coconut half-shells, which should be positioned toward the left, between two forklike branches of the tree root. In order to further enhance the decorative effect of the root and at the same time establish an attractive color contrast to the green leaves of the other plants, some large Pink Ammania are planted—in a loose pattern—behind it. The colloquial name "Cognac"

> **1 African Butterflyfish**

These fish are food specialists. Often it takes a very long time until they will accept artificial and dry foods in an aquarium.

> **2 Yellow Congo Tetra**

Adult yellow Congo Tetras like to be given flies or other insects as food.

> **3 African Butterfly Cichlid**

This species is characterized by a peaceful demeanor and very attractive coloration.

(sometimes used by European aquarists for this plant) refers to the light brownish, *lancifolious* leaves. This plant requires a fair amount of light. The open section in the foreground of the tank, as well as the space above the root, serve primarily as a "playground" for the fast-swimming Blue Congo Tetras. The more intensively colored males are adorned with long, drawn-out fins. As an alternative to Blue Congo Tetras, you can also use Yellow Congo Tetras (*Alestopetersius caudalis)* for this tank. The two back corners of the tank are planted with Bernier's Aponogeton, in groups that should border on the Pink Ammania. The African Water Ferns are arranged in a semicircle on both sides of Bernier's Aponogeton. This way the fern contributes to the "picture frame" effect around the root and at the same time it partially hides the side windows of the tank. The areas closest to the surface are the preferred location of Butterflyfish, which are known to be excellent "jumpers." For that reason, this tank must always have a properly fitted cover.

> *Two Blue Congo Tetras swim through typical African aquarium plants.*

In order to provide conditions that are as natural as possible for Butterflyfish, we can use two or three "stems" from a Centipede Tongavine (*Epipremnum pinnatum)*, standing next to the aquarium. The stems are manipulated to grow through an opening in the tank lid. Once inside the tank, the stems are attached to rubber suction caps located immediately above the water surface. Butterflyfish can then hide underneath the leaves of the vine, while waiting for food to fall onto the water surface.

Australian Tank

Rainbowfish are the characteristic inhabitants of Australian fresh waters. They are temperamental, very active fish.

Baseline Data

Because these are a very active fish, the tank size used here as an example—32 inches × 16 inches × 16 inches (80 × 40 × 40 cm)—should be used only for the smaller species. The pH value is adjusted to 7.0 and the water temperature is 75° F (24°C).

Layout

Decoration and Plants: The bottom substrate consists of sand that contains very small, well-rounded gravel, which should be slightly darker than the sand. As a centerpiece for this tank you can glue several flat rocks together to make a cave, attached to a slate tile of irregular shape. Such a cave is eagerly used by Australian Desert Gobies, which like to withdraw into hiding places like that. As an additional hiding opportunity you should place a 6-inch-long (15-cm-) bamboo tube (diameter 1½ inch [4 cm]) on to the tank bottom in the left far corner of the tank, flanked by two Longleaf Aponogeton. As additional background plants, you can use bunches (several individual stems held together) of Argentine Common Water Weed, following on from the location of the Aponogeton. Do not be confused by the designation "Argentine," because this plant does not only occur in South America but also in other parts of the world, such as in Australia. The right back corner of the tank is filled

> *The Australian Small Mutmat (or Glosso) forms dense, lawnlike covers.*

1 Neon Rainbow Fish

This species is frequently available in the aquarium trade. Its wine-red fins provide a magnificent contrast to the bluish body of males, which are more intensively colored than females. In the wild this species is found in jungle streams.

2 Australian Desert Goby

The male of this species is easily recognizable: dorsal and anal fin always display a striking coloration, not found in females. Moreover, females are slightly smaller. This species can survive completely unscathed in water temperatures as low as 28° F (–2°C).

with (Horned) Water Sprite. In front of the Water Sprite we plant group arrangements of Water Hyssop (*Bacopa monieri*). The remaining area of the tank is planted with the short Australian Water Hyssop. In time this plant will form a short, lawnlike cover over the substrate.

The areas above the rocky cave and above the Water Hyssop serve as open swimming spaces for rainbow fish, where they can race around totally unrestricted.

Fish: Rainbow fish—very much like barbs and tetras—seem to do well only when kept in large numbers. For that reason it is advisable to always purchase at least six specimens of each species. The designation "rainbow fish" comes from the eye-catching coloration feature of most of these fish, once they have reached adulthood. On the other hand, juvenile rainbow fish are often very plain, giving no indication of their eventual magnificent coloration. Anyone who wants to breed rainbow fish should attach a large bunch of Java Moss to a rock for the fish to use as spawning medium. Although Java Moss does not occur in Australia (it is found in the Philippines and on the Sunda Islands), in the interest of achieving successful breeding such minor "planting discrepancy" is probably "forgivable." After the fish have deposited a sufficient number of eggs in the moss, it can be removed effortlessly from the tank and placed into a separate rearing container. Although not native to Australia but to Papua-New Guinea, the Peacock Goby, also commonly known as Rainbow Gudgeon (*Tateurndina ocellicauda*), is often kept in an Australian tank.

North American Tank

Baseline Data

The advantage of a North American tank lies in the fact that in most instances you

> Mud Minnows are closely (phylogenetically) related to pikes.

can do without a heater, because the water temperature should generally be between 46 and 68° F (8 and 20° C), with a pH value of about 7.0. The suggestion for this theme aquarium is based on a tank with the dimensions 40 × 20 × 16 inches (100 × 50 × 40 cm).

Layout

Decoration and Plants: A mixture of sand and gravel should be used as bottom substrate. You are cautioned not to make any "aesthetic errors" when compiling the list of decorative materials required. For instance, "tropical" objects such as coconut shells, bamboo sticks, and palm leaves have no place in a North American Tank. On the left side of the tank we can place a large, gnarled root from which two branches extend (close to the tank bottom) all the way to the right side of the tank. About eight fist-size rocks are distributed along the bottom.

Four of them are grouped together on a piece of slate that is placed near the front window.

Two bunches of Common Watermoss are attached (using fishing line) to the root or to one of its branchlike extensions, respectively. The other two bunches of Watermoss are draped over the group of rocks, as well as over one individual rock on the right side of the tank. In the event Watermoss is not available from your aquarium shop, you may want to look for a very clean (unpolluted) body of water near your home for a few bunches of Watermoss—ideally together

American Redfin Shiners are among the most colorful cold-water fish. They prefer to live in large groups.

with the rocks they may be attached to with their rootlike structures. Once back at home, this moss is carefully rinsed under running water, and then it can be introduced into the aquarium. As an alternative, you can also use Liverwort *(Scapania undulate)* instead of common water moss; Liverwort looks virtually as attractive as water moss. Next to the root—essentially as background plants—you can place American Water Weed and Marsh Seedbox (also known as Water Purslane), arranged as a solid stand that extends into the right corner of the tank.

The Pearl Grass is scattered over the remaining open areas, essentially as ground cover. The open tank space above that provides the agile Redfin Shiners with ample swimming room. Since these are fish that have a high oxygen demand, the tank must be equipped with a powerful aerator . Similarly, lighting has to be fairly intense because plants such as Water Weed as well as Marsh Seedbox (= Water Purslane) require high light levels. If desired, a few Water Chestnut *(Trapa natans)* specimens can be permitted to drift on the water surface.

SHOPPING LIST

North American Tank

Fish

✔ 6 Red Shiner *(Notropis lutrensis)*, 7¼ inches (8 cm) each

✔ 4 Blue-spotted Sunfish *(Enneacanthus gloriosus)*, 7¼ inches (8 cm) each

✔ 2 Central Mudminnow *(Umbra limi)*, 4 inches (10 cm) each

Plants

✔ 30 stems American Water-weed *(Elodea canadensis)*

✔ 30 stems Marsh Seedbox *(Ludwigia palustris)*

✔ 4 large bunches Common Water Moss *(Fontinalis antipyretica)*

Questions and Answers About Interesting Behavior and Particular Species

Are Siamese Fighting Fish (*Betta splendens*) a potential threat to other tank inhabitants?

No, quite the contrary. Siamese Fighting Fish are very peaceful toward other fish. Even when they are attacked themselves by clearly smaller fish, Fighting Fish invariably see their salvation in retreat. Only when among themselves will males engage in fierce fighting, and in the event of insufficient flight opportunities, this often leads to the death of one of the combatants. For that reason you must never place two male Siamese Fighting Fish into the same tank.

Why is it not advisable to place Tiger Barbs (*Puntius sumatranus*) together with labyrinth fish or angelfish that have long, drawn-out (threadlike) pelvic fins?

The so-called "threads" of labyrinth fish and angelfish are in reality more or less the thin, long drawn-out pelvic fins of these fish. Hungry Tiger Barbs are always inclined to partially (or possibly even completely) nibble away these "threads." This behavior can possibly be explained in that the "threads" are being mistaken for worms, a popular type of food among Tiger Barbs. Unfortunately, fish "chewed-on" in this manner usually do not defend themselves, but instead attempt to flee, which then further stimulates the predatory instincts of the barbs.

I have observed that female Cockatoo Dwarf Cichlids (*Apistogramma caucatuoides*) frequently "suck" on the eggs of their clutch. Is that normal?

Yes. The mouths of dwarf cichlids as well as that of

> When "displaying," male Fighting Fish spread all their fins to a maximum extent.

other fish contain secretions that will kill microscopically small fungi and bacteria or inhibit their development. In essence, sucking on the eggs is an instinctive hygiene measure that removes harmful germs. At the same time, this increases the chance of hatching for the progeny, and so this behavior contributes to the survival of the species. In addition to sucking on eggs, female Cockatoo Dwarf Cichlids provide yet another type of care for their clutch, by creating a gentle water current that is directed over the eggs to wash away tiny dirt particles and to provide the eggs with oxygen-enriched water needed for normal development of the eggs.

What particular points do I need to pay special attention to when I want to keep Discus Cichlids (*Symphysodon aequifasciatus*)?

Discus Cichlids (generally referred to just as "Discus") are quite rightly considered to be delicate aquarium fish. In order to provide optimal care it requires a tank of at least 80 gallon (300 L) volume, with a constant water temperature of 80 to 86° F (27 to 30° C). In

addition, the water must be very soft and filtered over peat moss, with a pH value of 6.5. Moreover, the water surface should be covered with floating water plants. Discus are very peaceful and should not be kept together with highly active or aggressive species. Venezuelan Butterfly Cichlids are suitable companion species for Discus.

How old can aquarium fish get?

This is highly variable. Some species, for instance, killifish of the genus *Nothobranchius*, often do not get older than 10 to 12 months, and they reach sexual maturity at the age of two months. The situation is somewhat different with many large cichlids and catfish, where an age of 10 years is not unusual.

As a rule of thumb (which certainly has exceptions), one can assume that the greater the maximum size of a fish and the slower the normal growth during its youth, the higher the average longevity. You should take longevity into account when you decide what species of fish to include in your tank.

Observing Your Fish

Observing the behavior of fish provides not only a lot of fun but it is also highly educational. For maximum enjoyment it is advisable to adhere to the following guidelines:

➤ Avoid creating a disturbance when observing the aquarium. Do not knock against the glass or make any sudden movements that would cause the fish to flee for cover.

➤ Take detailed notes about the behavior of your fish. In time this will enable you to better understand their behavior, and will then also help you to react and respond to it correctly. For instance, suddenly occurring, atypical behavior can be the first sign of the onset of a disease.

➤ If you are specifically interested in fish breeding you can transfer your fish immediately to a separate tank for spawning, once you have observed their courtship behavior.

➤ If you have other pets (e.g., dogs or cats) in your household, you should make sure that they can't disturb your fish.

Bold page numbers indicate illustrations.

Addresses
Associations / Clubs
Most, if not all, major metropolitans areas in North America, Great Britain, Australia, etc. have aquarium clubs and similar associations, invariably with appropriate e-mail contact addresses or—in many cases—their own web sites. Comprehensive listings are found in
➤ "The Meeting Place," for details see latest issue of *Tropical Fish Hobbyist* Magazine.

➤ The International Federation of Online Clubs and Aquatic Societies (http://www.ifocas.fsworld.co.uk).
➤ Northeast Council of Aquarium Societies (http://www.northeastcounjcil.org/html/).
➤ The Canadian Association of Aquarium Clubs (http://www.caoac.on.ca).

Organizations Specializing in Certain Aquarium Fish Groups:
➤ American Livebearer Association (http://www.livebearer.org)
➤ American Cichlid Association (http://www.cichlid.org)
➤ The Angelfish Society (http://www.theangelfishsociety.org)
➤ American Killifish Association (http://www.aka.org)

Aquarium Keeping on the Internet
Comprehensive information relating to all aspects of aquarium keeping is available from the Internet, principally through the web sites of major associations (see above). In addition, global searches using some of the major "search engines" (Google, Lycos, AltaVista, etc.) will provide a wealth of relevant information on aquarium-related topics.

Questions on aquarium keeping can be directed to
Your local aquarium shop, global subject search on the Internet, or the web sites of the organizations listed above.

Insurance
Contact your insurance broker about what major insurers provide adequate cover for damages (water, electrical, personal, and property).

Books
➤ Nick Fletcher et al., *What Fish?: A Buyer's Guide to Tropical Fish.* Hauppauge, NY: Barron's Educational Series, Inc., 2006.
➤ Petra Kölle, *Compass Guides: 300 Questions about the Aquarium.* Hauppauge, NY: Barron's Educational Series, Inc., 2007.
➤ Tristan Lougher, *What Fish?: A Buyer's Guide to Marine Fish.* Hauppauge, NY: Barron's Educational Series, Inc., 2006.

Aquarium Magazines and Journals

➤ FAMA— *Freshwater and Marine Aquarium*, BowTie Inc., Irvine, California 92618

➤ *Tropical Fish Hobbyist*, TFH Publications, Inc., Neptune, New Jersey

➤ Regional aquarium magazines and journals in Germany, Great Britain, Italy, and other countries (check the Internet for details)

The photographers:

Aquapress: pp. 3, 11 (left), 20, 23 (all), 24, 31 (top), 33 (right), 37 (left), 40 (left), 47 center; Giel: pp. 6, 14 cover 1; Gutjahr: pp. 8 (right), 31 (center), 61; Hartl: pp. 54, 55; Hecker: pp. 2, 16, 17, cover 2, cover 4 (center); Kahl: pp. 9, 10, 11 (center), 11 (right), 18, 19, 21 (all), 26, 27, 29, 35, 36, 37 (right), 38 (center), 39, 40 (all), 44, 45, 46, 47 (top), 47 (bottom), 48, 49, 50 (left), 59 (center) Lamboj: p. 33 (left); Linke: p. 8 (left); Lucas: p. 38; Peither: pp. 7, 22, 51, cover 4 (left); Reinhard: pp. 7, 22, 51, cover 4 (left); Reinhard Tierfoto: pp. 8 (center), 28, 32; Schmida: p. 53 (left); Schmidbauer: pp. 2, 30, 31(bottom), 34, 42, 64, cover 4 (right); Staeck: p. 38 (right); Werner: p. 53 (right).

Author

Axel Gutjahr has been fascinated by the care and breeding of fish since his childhood days. His passion was further enhanced through his tertiary studies in animal breeding and agricultural economics. Apart from his general widespread interest in tropical fish in general, his particular interest is focused on coldwater fish species and the care and maintenance of garden ponds. On the subject of aquarium keeping, Axel Gutjahr has already authored several successful books, and has published numerous articles in specialist journals.

Translated from the German by U. Erich Friese

Original German title: *Aquarien Einrichten*
© Copyright 2006 by Gräfe und Unzer Verlag GmbH, Munich.

All inquiries should be addressed to:
Barron's Educational Series, Inc.
250 Wireless Boulevard
Hauppauge, NY 11788
www.barronseduc.com

ISBN-13: 978-0-7641-3740-2
ISBN-10: 0-7641-3740-9

Library of Congress Control Number: 2006933017

Printed in China
9 8 7 6 5 4 3 2 1

My Aquarium

➤ **Type of Aquarium:** _____

These are the fish I keep:

➤ _____
_____
_____

Size and Volume:

➤ _____
_____
_____

This is how I feed them:

➤ _____
_____
_____

Regular Maintenance Tasks:

➤ _____
_____
_____

These are the water plants I keep:

➤ _____
_____
_____

Technical Equipment:

➤ _____
_____
_____

LESS IS MORE

You must keep only as many fish as your aquarium can actually support. Calculating the final stocking density must always be based on the final, adult size of the fish species.. Moreover, you also have to take into consideration the water volume displaced by bottom substrate and tank decorations.

Well-being of Aquarium Fish

SENSIBLE DECORATION

The decorative items used must always fit thematically to the fish and plants in the respective aquarium type. For instance, coconut half-shells, palm leaves, and bamboo do not belong in a coldwater aquarium used for keeping North American or European fish and plants.

FEEDING CORRECTLY

Fully grown fish should be fed twice a day. Once a week, insert a fasting day. This prevents the fish from becoming too fat and it also enhances their agility and well-being.

EFFECTIVE TECHNOLOGY

It is always advisable to start out with aqua support technology that is easy to install an provides sufficient capacity to maintain the aquarium. The equipment acquired must b optimal effectiveness and at the same time the lowest possible energy consumption.